Savvy

DRAW YOUR OWN

Nature

ZENDOODLES

By Abby Huff

Illustrated by Pimlada Phuapradit

CAPSTONE PRESS
a capstone imprint

Savvy Books are published by Capstone Press, a Capstone imprint
1710 Roe Crest Drive
North Mankato, Minnesota 56003
www.mycapstone.com

Library of Congress Cataloging-in-Publication Data
Names: Huff, Abby, 1991– author. | Phuapradit, Pimlada, illustrator.
Title: Draw your own nature zendoodles / by Abby Huff ; illustrated by Pimlada Phuapradit.
Description: North Mankato, Minnesota : Capstone Press, 2017. | Series: Savvy.
   Draw your own zendoodles | Audience: Ages 9–13. | Audience: Grades 4 to 8.
Identifiers: LCCN 2016044393 | ISBN 9781515748434 (library binding) | ISBN
   9781515748502 (ebook pdf)
Subjects: LCSH: Nature in art—Juvenile literature. | Drawing—Technique—Juvenile
   literature. | Handicraft for children—Juvenile literature.
Classification: LCC NC825.N34 H84 2017 | DDC 743/.83—dc23
LC record available at https://lccn.loc.gov/2016044393

Editorial Credits
Bobbie Nuytten, designer; Jo Miller, media researcher; Laura Manthe, premedia specialist

Photo Credits
Capstone Studio: Karon Dubke, 7 (all), 44-47 (all), Shutterstock: AgriTech, 30, Aleoks, 38, artjazz, 16, BOONCHUAY PROMJIAM, 18, Dark Moon Pictures, 36, Galyna_, 38, gresei, 14, Lostry7, 25, mama_mia, 28, robert_s, 40, Rolau Elena, 22, ULKASTUDIO, 12, Viktora, 36, Zadorozhnyi Viktor, 39; Backgrounds: Shutterstock: aopsan, arigato, CCat82, donatas1205, happykanppy, Lana Veshta, macknimal, Mikhail Pogosov, Nik Merkulov, Only background, Piotr Zajc, Ratana21, redstone, siriak kaewgorn, Turbojet, Vadim Georgiev

Crafts created by Lori Blackwell and Tyson J. Schultz

Printed in the United States of America.
010062S17

Table of Contents

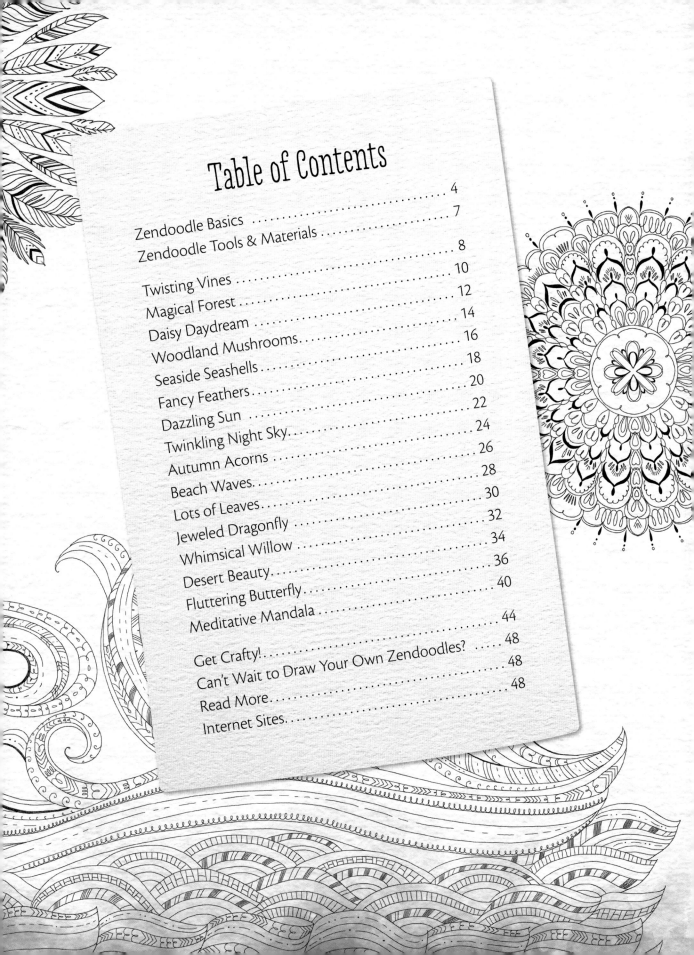

Zendoodle Basics 4
Zendoodle Tools & Materials 7

Twisting Vines 8
Magical Forest 10
Daisy Daydream 12
Woodland Mushrooms 14
Seaside Seashells 16
Fancy Feathers 18
Dazzling Sun 20
Twinkling Night Sky 22
Autumn Acorns 24
Beach Waves 26
Lots of Leaves 28
Jeweled Dragonfly 30
Whimsical Willow 32
Desert Beauty 34
Fluttering Butterfly 36
Meditative Mandala 40

Get Crafty! 44
Can't Wait to Draw Your Own Zendoodles? 48
Read More 48
Internet Sites 48

Zendoodle Basics

So, what are zendoodles? A zendoodle is an intricate design built up from simple patterns. It's also a beautiful and relaxing way to express yourself on paper. There's no true "right" or "wrong" way to make zendoodles. When in doubt, let your imagination be your guide. Sometimes, though, it's helpful to know a few basics. Here are some fundamentals to start you on the path to calm and creative.

Patterns

Zendoodles may look complicated, but they're created from basic patterns. Make patterns by repeating and layering different strokes and shapes. Using multiple designs in a zendoodle gives it its signature tangled style.

Shapes and Motifs

Small shapes and motifs (a fancy word for recurring forms and elements) can be used to help fill a zendoodle. Use teardrops, fans, circles, flowers, and more. Try drawing a cluster of shapes in your zendoodle or spread them out. Decorate them with dots, lines, or a pattern for an elaborate look.

Adding Patterns

Adding patterns is the most fun and calming part of the zendoodle process. There are two main methods. Try both to see which you like best.

Sectioned
Divide your drawing with lines. Fill each section with a pattern.

Free-formed
Let your patterns overlap and run into each other. When you're done, it should be hard to tell where one pattern begins and another ends.

Object Zendoodles

Zendoodles don't have to resemble anything. You can simply fill a page with elegant designs. Other times, it's fun to make your zendoodle into a recognizable object, like a flower or leaf. When you're working with an object, try experimenting with these two methods.

Positive space

Draw inside the object. This is using the positive space — the space occupied by a subject. Decorate within the lines using adorable details and doodles.

Negative space

Draw around the object. This is using the negative space — the space around a subject. For maximum impact, don't add any details inside the object. Leave it completely blank for a striking graphic look.

Warm Up

Loosen your wrist and relax your mind. Get started with zigzags, squiggles, dots, curls, and more.

Zendoodle Tools & Materials

If you have a pencil and a scrap of paper, you're ready to zendoodle! But it can be fun to try out other supplies too. Here are a few essentials to keep in your toolbox.

Pencils

The most basic doodle tool. Try a mechanical pencil for consistently precise, even lines.

Paper

A page from your notebook can do in a pinch. For best results, use drawing or sketch paper. The thicker paper will hold up better to erasing and marking. Paper also comes in different textures. Generally, it'll be easier to doodle on a smooth surface.

Pens

Pens are perfect for polished zendoodles. Splurge on drawing pens for smoother, high quality lines. Look for archival or pigment ink pens. The special ink won't smudge or fade, so it'll keep your design looking pretty.

Colors

Zendoodles are bold in black and white, but color adds a whole new dimension. Use colored pencils for a soft look. Try markers and colored pens for dramatic color. There are many options to choose from. Enjoy experimenting!

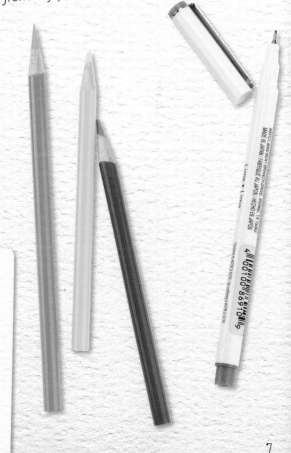

Quick and Easy Zendoodles

Not feeling confident in your drawing abilities? Want to start doodling right away? Head to **capstonekids.com**. There you can download sheets with blank outlines. Simply print the page and you're ready to go. Add exciting patterns and designs to make it your own.

Twisting Vines

Unwind with curly, delicate vines. Fill the page top to bottom with strands of these climbing plants. They also make perfect borders around a page. Add some buds or blooming flowers for a spring feel.

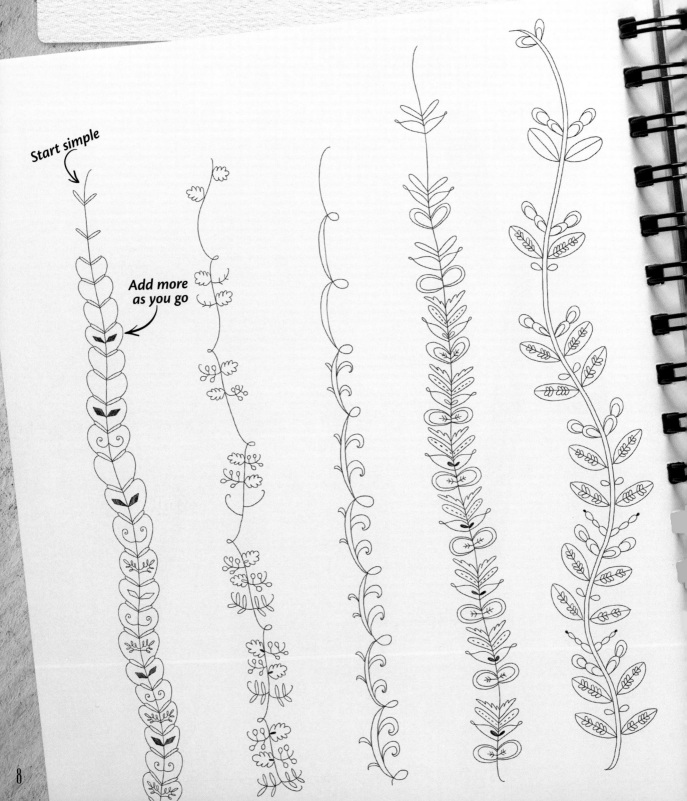

Start simple

Add more as you go

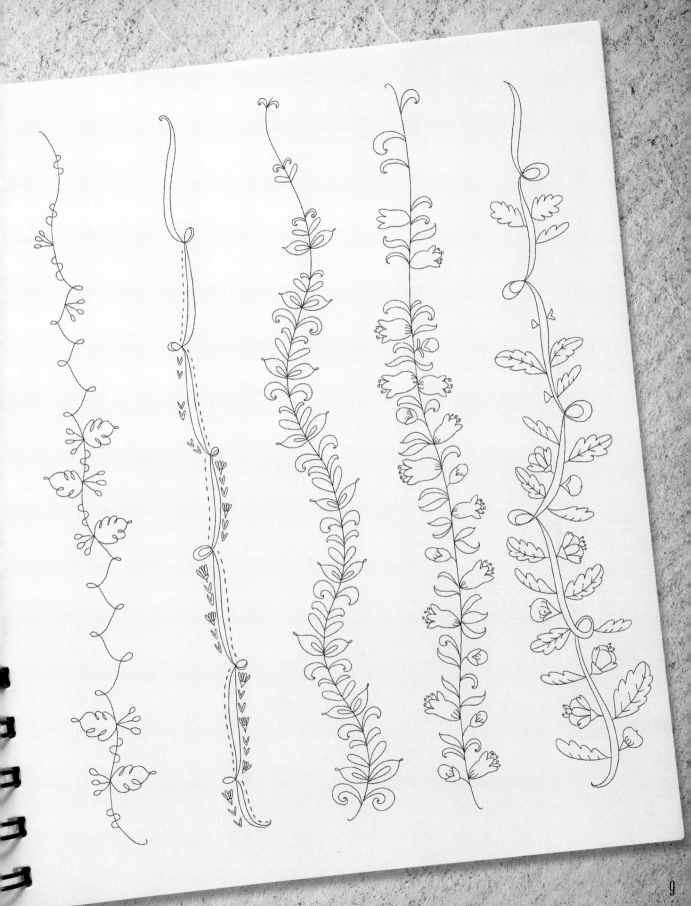

Magical Forest

Create your own forest. All you need to do is start with a simple trunk. Add a few branches and sketch the outline of the foliage. Fill it with a leafy pattern. Or, skip adding branches. Make a swirling pattern starting from the trunk instead. Enjoy your enchanting trees!

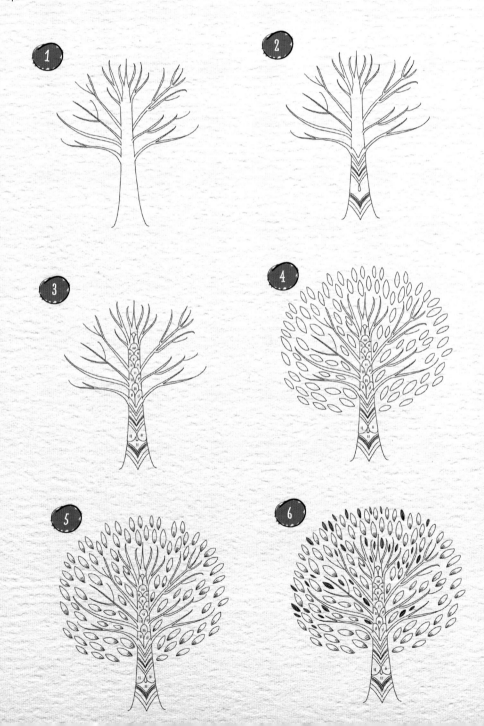

Daisy Daydream

Nothing is more classic than a simple daisy. Make your flowers anything but ordinary with a few frills and rounded shapes. Once you've gotten the hang of it, try filling the page with a field of daisies in bloom. Add some leaves to complete your design.

Woodland Mushrooms

These small fungi like to stay tucked away in cool, shaded places. Make your mushrooms stand out with scalloped patterns. Or try adding spots to the mushroom cap. Leave the spots blank and doodle all around them. Your zendoodle will be quirky-cute!

Color It!

Turn your zendoodles into custom coloring pages. If you drew in pencil, trace over your design with black pen. A waterproof or archival quality pen is best. The ink won't bleed if you color over it. Now you're ready to start coloring with your favorite tool. Or, before you color, make photocopies of your zendoodle. That way you can color it again and again. You could even host a coloring party for you and your friends!

Seaside Seashells

Create your own collection of seashells. Start with simple snail shells. Then try clamshells, conchs, and more. Mix flowing patterns inspired by the sea with angular patterns for an interesting contrast.

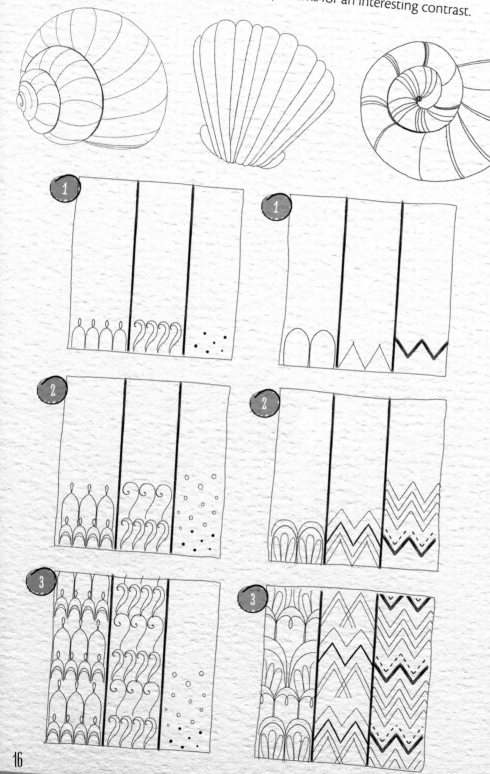

Fancy Feathers

Bring a fun boho vibe to your zendoodles with these feathers. Build your pattern starting from the center of the feather. Or, pick two or three patterns and repeat them throughout.

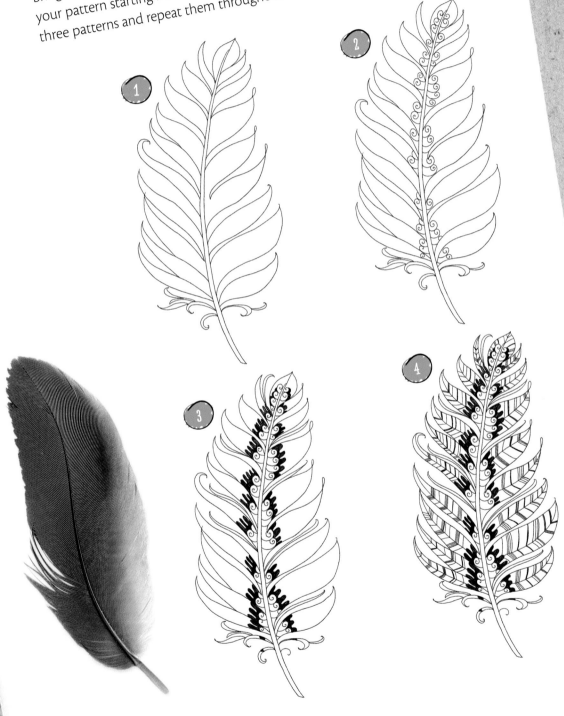

Dazzling Sun

Cloudy day? You can always soak in some sunshine with this zendoodle sun. Start with a circle and let your imagination run wild. For a fresh look, use dashes of various lengths to create sunrays. Try adding small charms and embellishments to the lines for an even more creative approach.

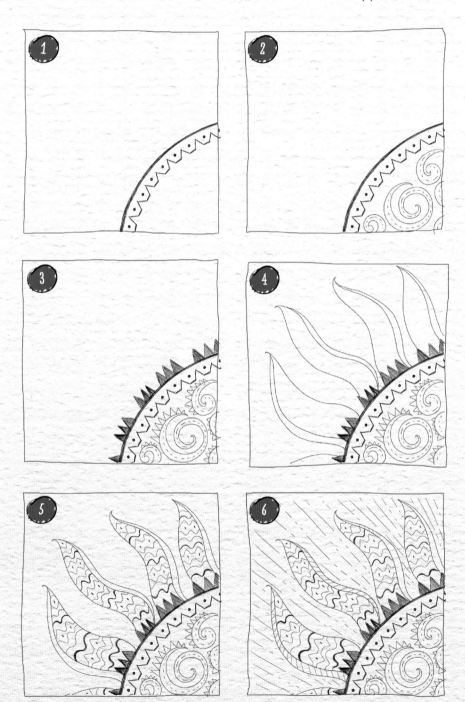

Twinkling Night Sky

Make a wish on these magical moon and stars. Draw a crescent shape and layer patterns inside. The stacked designs will create one gorgeous zendoodle. Adding simple borders around the stars make them shine bright.

Nighttime Twist

Use black or blue paper for a cool new look. Just switch out your pencil for gel pens — the color will pop against the dark background. White, silver, and gold gel pens work especially well. Try white colored pencils for a softer, more feathery look.

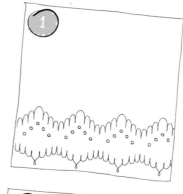

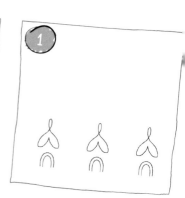

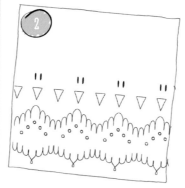

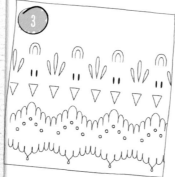

Autumn Acorns

Say hello to cooler weather and harvest colors with cute acorns.
Draw a cluster of nuts or put a few on a twisty oak branch.
Fill the branch with swirly shapes to add woody texture.

Beach Waves

Get swept up in these soothing zendoodle waves. Make swirling, swooping, and curling strokes. Then begin adding patterns. Fill in all the lines or leave some blank to create a hypnotizing flow.

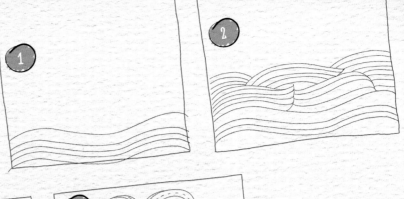

Creative Colored Pens

Freshen up your zendoodles and draw with colored pens! Switch out your black pen for bright neons, cool pastels, or sparkly glitter gel inks.

Here are a few ways to use your colored pens:

- Use one colored pen for the whole zendoodle.
- Pick a couple of colors. Doodle a large section in one color. Draw the next section in a new color. Alternate throughout the zendoodle.
- Draw the large shapes in your zendoodle using one color. Use other colors to make the patterns.
- Doodle in pen. Then take out colored pencils and color in your design. Choose hues similar to the pen for a coordinated look.

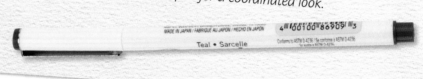

Lots of Leaves

Get started with these lovely leaves, then challenge yourself. Take your sketchbook outside and let nature inspire you. Look for interesting shapes. Design new leaf zendoodles that express your unique style.

29

Jeweled Dragonfly

Capture the spirit of this quick insect onto your page. Add cool patterns to the body and each section of the wing. Finish it with out-of-the-box colors to recreate a dragonfly's shimmering hues.

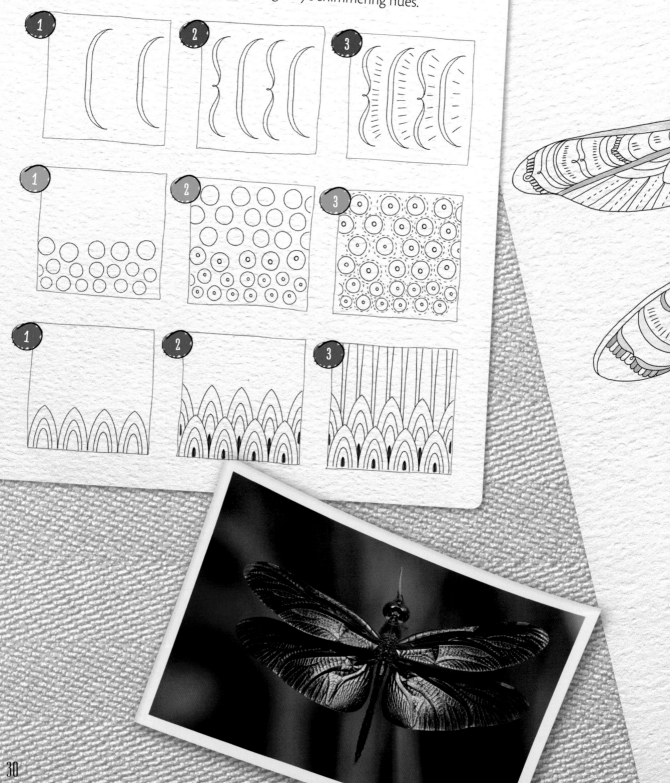

Whimsical Willow

Delicate dangling zendoodles create the perfect fantasy tree. Begin by drawing a thin trunk and branches. From the branches, add gently curved lines. Decorate some of the lines by adding little charms to the end. Add embellishments along the entire line for a fuller look.

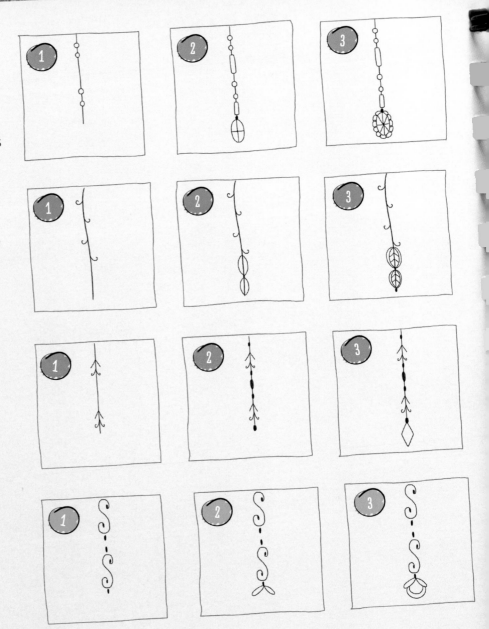

Charmed

Vertical doodles become extra sweet with a few additions. Draw a charm at the end of a dangle zendoodle to give it some weight and style. Experiment with the ones below or create charms that reflect your personality and interests.

Desert Beauty

The natural world is full of elegance — even in the desert. Burst patterns and pointy zigzags make these prickly plants extra pretty. Add a bloom for a pop of color. A contrasting color like red or deep pink will help the flower stand out.

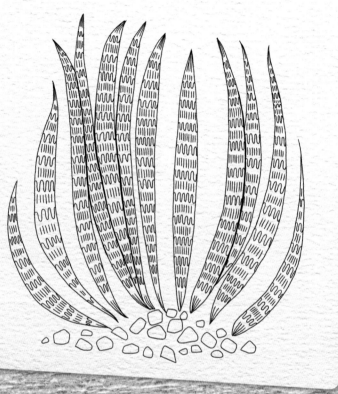

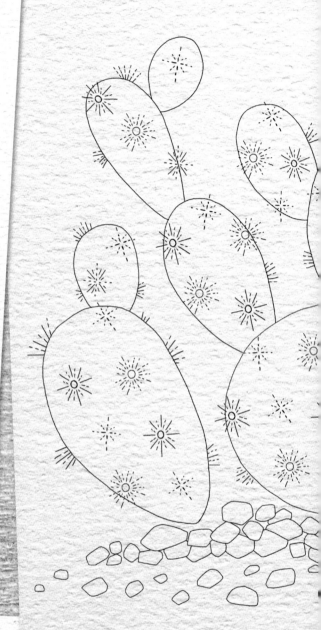

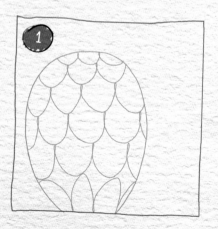

Fluttering Butterfly

Transform your doodles into a beautiful butterfly! Start with one of the outlines provided or sketch your own. Section the wing with curving lines and long ovals. Then have fun experimenting with patterns. Try an unexpected floral design, natural spots, or whatever feels right as you flutter it up.

Adding Watercolor

For a soft splash of color, try watercolors. Start with thick drawing or watercolor paper. With a large brush, apply a thin layer of water to the page. Load your brush with watercolor and paint onto the wet paper. Create the general shape of your design or try an abstract form. Dry completely before doodling over it with pencil or pen.

Meditative Mandala

Get zen with a calming mandala. These intricate, circular drawings only look difficult. Take it one layer at a time and you can easily create your own. Remember to relax as you draw. Before you know it, you'll have an elaborate design and a peaceful mind.

Making a Mandala

Construct a grid to keep your mandala balanced. Use a protractor to measure out even sections. Try 15 degrees to start. Then make layers using a compass. Place the needle in the center and draw circles with various diameters. Use your completed grid as a guide to creating symmetrical designs. Draw petals, triangles, and more in the sections, repeating them around the circle.

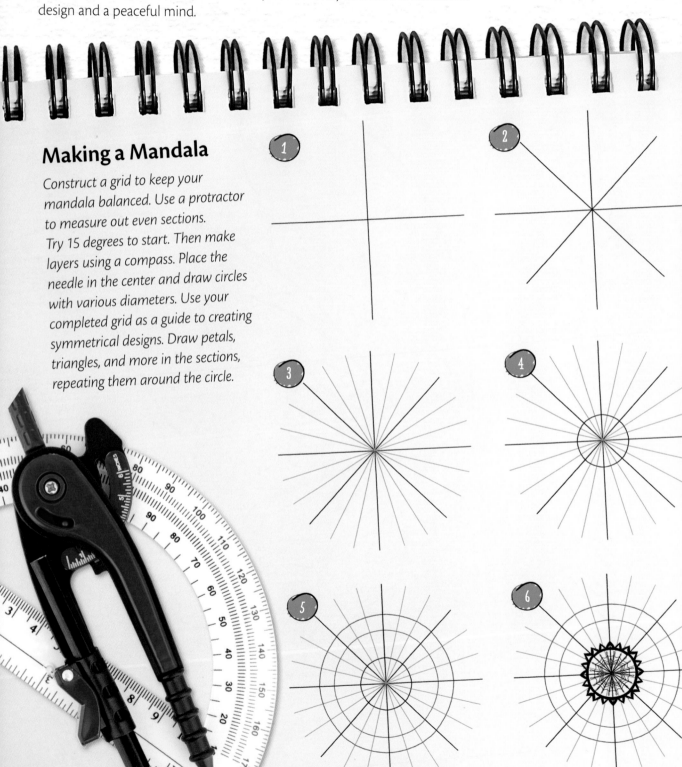

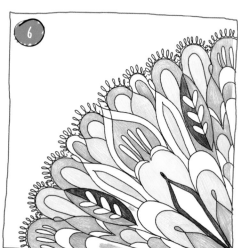

Get Crafty!

Zendoodles don't have to stay in your sketchbook. These fancy doodles are perfect for decorating and adding flair to everyday items. All you need is a little creativity. So if you're feeling artsy, try a variety of projects and crafts that'll showcase your zendoodles to the world. Be inspired to create your own DIY masterpiece — take your zendoodles off the page!

Easy Stained Glass

Bring color to a window or wall with this unique piece. Start with a photo frame. Throw away the backing and clean the glass with rubbing alcohol. Place a finished zendoodle under the glass. Use bright permanent markers to trace and color in your design. To protect your art, brush a layer of decoupage glue over the dried marker. Finish by attaching the glass to the frame with industrial-strength glue. It may be faux stained glass, but it's a truly vibrant decoration!

Pretty Planters

Dress up a simple flowerpot with zendoodles. Start with an inexpensive clay pot. You can find them at home improvement stores, garden centers, or craft stores. Doodle directly onto the pot with oil-based paint pens. If you want more color, apply a layer of acrylic paint in your favorite hue before drawing.

Zendoodle Shoes

Plain white canvas shoes become fabulous with zendoodles! Sketch your design first. Then go over it with markers or pens. Using fine-tip markers will make tiny details easier. When you're done, spray on a waterproof sealant in a well-ventilated area. It'll protect your artsy new kicks.

Styling Shades

Bring some attitude to your summer look. Use pens to decorate your sunglasses for a quick craft. For a more permanent design, start by unscrewing the sunglasses' temples (the parts that go over your ears). Trace them onto a piece of paper. Doodle in the outline and then cut it out. Apply a thin layer of decoupage glue to the temples and stick on the cutouts. Coat with dimensional glue for a polished look.

Tumbling Leaves Mobile

Bring a touch of natural elegance to your room. Cut leaves out of paper or use real leaves collected on a nature walk. Decorate using your favorite markers. If you use real leaves, dip them in melted wax or seal them with self-adhesive laminate paper. This will keep them preserved so you can enjoy your mobile all year round. Hang your finished designs from a branch with clear string. It'll create the illusion of the leaves being caught on a gentle breeze.

Picture-Perfect Frame

Display your favorite memories with pizzazz! Pick a flat wooden frame to decorate. It will be easiest to work on. Try building layers of patterns around the frame. For a laid-back look, focus on one or two large zendoodles. A zendoodle flower with leaves or vines crawling up the side would be a very sweet, natural design.

Glamorous Shells

Accentuate the natural beauty of a seashell with a few well-placed doodles. Try out simple, repetitive patterns so the details don't get muddled. For a graceful design, work in the lines of the shell. Give your completed shell to a friend or use it to add a bit of beachy style to your decor.

Can't wait to draw your own zendoodles?

Visit **capstonekids.com** to download blank outlines. Simply print and start doodling.
Add your own unique curls, twirls, and tangles!

Read More

Corfee, Stephanie. *Free Spirit Doodles*. Doodle with Attitude. North Mankato, Minn.: Capstone Press, 2016.

Marbaix, Jane. *Zentangle for Kids*. New York: Sterling Children's Books, 2015.

Schwake, Susan. *Art Lab for Kids: 52 Creative Adventures in Drawing, Painting, Printmaking, Paper, and Mixed Media-For Budding Artists of All Ages*. Lab Series. Beverly, Mass.: Quarry Books, 2012.

Internet Sites

FactHound offers a safe, fun way to find Internet sites related to this book. All of the sites on FactHound have been researched by our staff.

Here's all you do:
Visit www.facthound.com
Type in this code: 9781515748434